Series: *Language, Media & Education Studies*

Edited by: Marcel Danesi & Leonard G. Sbrocchi

1. M. Danesi, *Interpreting Advertisements. A Semiotic Guide*
2. M. Angenot, *Critique of Semiotic Reason*
3. S. Feigenbaum, *The Intermediate Sign in the System of French and Hebrew Verbs*
4. A. Bailin, *Metaphor and the Logic of Language Use*
5. C.D.E. Tolton, ed., *The Cinema of Jean Cocteau*
6. C. Madott Kosnik, *Primary Education: Goals, Processes and Practices*
7. F. Nuessel, *The Esperanto Language*
8. M.G. Guido, *The Acting Reader*
9. F. Ratto, *Hobbes tra scienza della politica e teoria delle passioni*
10. S. Battestini, *African Writing and Text*
11. T. A. Sebeok, *Essays in Semiotics I: Life Signs*
12. T. A. Sebeok, *Essays in Semiotics I: Culture Signs*
13. A. Ponzio and S. Petrilli, *Philosophy of Language, art and aswerability in Mikhail Baktin*

Cover: Luciano Ponzio, *Deferrals and differences*
acrylic on wood, 100 x 66,6 cm, 2000.

Augusto Ponzio and Susan Petrilli

Philosophy of Language, Art and Answerability in Mikhail Bakhtin

LEGAS

New York Ottawa Toronto

Canadian Cataloguing in Publication Data

Main entry under title:

Augusto Ponzio and Susan Petrilli
Philosophy of language,
art and answerability in Mikhail Baktin

(Language, Media & Education Studies; 13)
Includes bibliographical references
ISBN 1-894508-08-4

1. Bakhtin, M.M. (Mikhail Mikhailovich), 1895-1975
2. Literature--Philosophy. 3. Language and languages--Philosophy.
4. Semiotics and literature. I. Petrilli, Susan II. Title. III. Series.

PG2947.B3P65 2000 801 C00-900885-3

For further information and for orders:

LEGAS

P. O. Box 040328
Brooklyn, New York
USA 11204

68 Kamloops Ave.
Ottawa, Ontario
K1V 7C9

2908 Dufferin Street
Toronto, Ontario
M6B 3S8

Printed and bound in Canada

Contents

Foreword

An author's importance becomes obvious when his writings engender multiple and different readings. Mikhail M. Bakhtin is one such author.

His research came to light after years of silence and since then numerous readings have been dedicated to him from varying perspectives. Moreover, the many different aspects of his work were discovered and published after his death, gradually, and not even in the order of their composition. There are texts from the early 1920s which only just recently have come to our attention. Their importance is such that they have thrown new light over the whole corpus of Bakhtin's research.

We must also add that Bakhtin's thought ranges over different fields on its own account, and now, beyond this, his research has been transported into disciplinary areas which he had not faced directly, and is used to deal with new problems.

With the present little volume in two parts, the authors wish to contribute to the ongoing process of rereading Bakhtin in a new light.

His work has been the object of our studies in several other publications, devoted to his research and writings, including monographs in the case of Augusto Ponzio. And yet, it continues to be necessary to return to our own interpretations and review them, rethink and develop them and sometimes even reorient them in different perspectives not solely in the light of texts which have only just recently been "discovered", but of texts which are already familiar to us.

Therefore, this booklet is an attempt at viewing the whole course of Bakhtin's research with reference to his early writings of 1919-1924 on the one hand, and at examining the import of his work from the perspective of "philosophy of language", on the other.

What emerges most strongly at an overall gaze is that however one wishes to use Bakhtinian thought and wherever one wishes to apply it, his main concern lies with what we might call philosophy or theory of literature and "philosphy of language", to use an expression chosen by Bakhtin himself to denominate his research.

Philosophy of literature and philosophy of language are inseparable just as it is difficult, if not impossible, to separate what belongs to Bakhtin from his collaborators Valentin N. Voloshinov and Pavel N. Medvedev in works from the 1920s signed by the latter. In addition to being interconnected, Bakhtin's philosophy of language and philosophy of literature share roots in the same territory, that of moral philosophy. Originally, Bakhtin was interested in moral philosophy dwelling particularly on the problem of responsibility. Indeed, in his earliest paper of 1919 which was turned to questions relating to art (in line with the journal where it was published, an art journal), he had already connected the problem of art to the problem of responsibility.

Bakhtin was not concerned with limited responsibility as delineated within the context of identity. He had no interest for identity. When he analyses art, he is not concerned with the artist's identity, nor is he interested in the identity of a literary genre or of a literary trend when analysing literary texts. By the same token, Bakhtin is not concerned with the identity of language in his studies on problems related to language. The "Bakhtinian revolution" consists in the shift of attention from identity to alterity in relation to all these problems and disciplinary fields.

Bakhtin is interested in responsibility understood as answering to and for the other, without alibis. He is interested in showing how the value of other and not of I is aesthetically productive. He analyses the word in order to underscore the presence in it of another word, which renders it internally dialogic. He deals with linguistic problems in order to demonstrate how centrifugal forces operate alongside the centripetal forces that determine a language's identity, and which continually render language other with respect to itself. Bakhtin expresses this shift in attention in the direction of otherness with the term "meta-": and speaks of his studies on language with the term "metalinguistics".

The properly philosophical orientation of Bakhtin's philosophy of language is determined by his shift in focus beyond the boundaries of identity. His philosophy of literature also moves in the same direction for it too transcends the limits of literary theory and criticism confined to identity — linguistic, cultural, national identity, the identity of discourse genre. When researching into signs Bakhtin does not limit his attention to verbal signs but also shifts towards nonverbal signs, and when a question of denominating his work on signs he refuses the term "semiotics" (and explicitly so in his notes from the 1970s). In this case, too, we must speak of "metasemiotics".

The two parts forming this booklet intend to highlight the role of alterity in the general project of Bakhtin's conceptualizations: the first makes a study of Bakhtin's philosophy of literature, the second considers the contribution that may come from Bakhtinian categories for renewal within the field of philosophy of language. These two parts are closely related. And this is not only determined by the way they have been conceived and written, but above all by the fact that philosophy of literature and philosophy of language are the two interconnected faces of the same unitary project subtending Bakhtinian research when we consider it as an accomplished whole. If, on the contrary, we wish to consider Bakhtin's work as it presents itself on the move, as it develops, in its most basic impulse, there is no doubt that the overall course of his research may be considered as belonging to the field of (meta-semiotically renewed) moral philosophy.

Augusto Ponzio

From Moral Philosophy to Philosophy of Literature:

Directions in Bakhtin's Research from 1919 to 1929

An early text by Mikhail M. Bakhtin from the 1920s entitled "K filosofii postupka" (Toward a philosophy of the act), was only published in Russia as late as 1986 in the volume *Filosofija i sočiologija nauki i tekniki: Ezegodnik 1984-85,* edited by S. G. Bocharov (pp. 82-138).[1] This text is of great interest not only because of its intrinsic theoretical value, but also because it yields an understanding of the overall sense of Bakhtin's research as it stretches into the first half of the 1970s. Furthermore, it is closely related to the first chapter of another text written during the early 1920s, "Autor i geroj vi estetičeskoj dejatel'nosti" (Author and hero in aesthetic activity), it too only published later —in 1979— in the volume *Estetika slovesnogo tvorčestva*[2] (cf. Bakhtin 1979). However, this chapter was not published in a complete version; the first section was excluded having been considered too fragmentary and was only published in 1986 with "K filosofii postupka", in the same volume. The connection between these two texts, "K filosofii postupka" and "Autor i geroj vi estetičeskoj dejatel'nosti" (and in particular the first section of the latter) is immediately obvious: both are part of the same research project where "Autor i geroj vi estetičeskoj dejatel'nosti" is the continuation and development of "K filosofii postupka", and both privilege the same literary text as their object of analysis, the poem *Razluka* (*Parting*), by Pushkin.

Toward a Philosophy of the Act, which was only the beginning of a vast philosophical project designed to produce a volume in moral philosophy, consists of two large fragments: what is probably an introduc-

---

[1]Translated into English as *Toward a Philosophy of the Act,* 1993; and into Italian as "Per una filosofia dell'azione responsabile" (Toward a Philosophy of Responsible Action), first presented with other writings by Bakhtin and his Circle (in Bakhtin 1995 et alii), and subsequently completely revised and published as an independent volume (cf. Bakhtin 1998).

[2]This volume was translated into Italian in 1988 which also excluded the first chapter in question. This, however, has now been translated into Italian from Russian and published in a volume edited by A. Ponzio and P. Jachia, *Bachtin e ...,* 1993, under the title "L'autore e l'eroe nell'attività estetica. Frammento del primo capitolo". As to the English edition, included in the volume *Art and Answerability,* 1990, edited by M. Holquist and V. Liapunov, "Author i geroj vi estetičeskoj dejatel' nosti " has been published as "Author and Hero in Aesthetic Activity", while the first chapter of this text is placed at the end under the title "Supplementary Section" (cf. Bakhtin 1990: 208-231).

tion to the project (with a few initial pages missing); and a section entitled "I", as established by Bakhtin himself.

In the introductory fragment, Bakhtin considers the problem of the possibility of capturing the moment of "transitiveness" and "eventness" (*sobytijnost'*) (cf. p. 1)[3] of the act in its valuableness and unity of actual becoming and self-determination. As soon as the sense of such an act is determined from a theoretical —scientific, philosophical, historiographical— or aesthetic viewpoint, it loses its character of unique and self-determined event, a truly lived act and assumes a generic value, an abstract meaning. A division is created between two mutually impervious worlds: the world of life and the world of culture; and yet we exist in the first even when we cognize, contemplate and create, that is, when we build a world in which life is the object of a given domain of culture. These two worlds are united by the unique event of the act of our activity, of living experience, being the unity of two-sided answerability: answerability with respect to objective meaning, that is, with respect to a content relative to the objective unity of a domain of culture, which Bakhtin calls "special answerability", and answerability with respect to the unique event-ness of the act, which he calls "moral answerability" (cf. p. 2-3). For unity among these two kinds of answerability, "special answerability must be brought into communion with the unitary and unique moral answerability as a constituent moment in it. That is the only way whereby the pernicious non-fusion and non-interpenetratoin of culture and life could be surmounted" (p. 3).

This is the same problem dealt with in what is generally believed to be the first writing ever published by Bakhtin, "Art and Answerability", of 1919, that is, the problem of the relationship between art and life, with a solution perspected in terms that are similar:

> The three domains of human culture —science, art, and life — gain unity only in the individual person who integrates them into his own unity. This union, however, may become mechanical, external. And, unfortunately, that is exactly what most often happens. [...] But what guarantees the inner connection of the constituent elements of a person? Only the unity of answerability. I have to answer with my own life for what I have experienced and understood in art, so that everything I have experienced and understood would not remain ineffectual in my life. But answerability entails guilt, or liability to blame. It is not only mutual answerability that art and life must assume, but also mutual liability to blame. [...] The poet must remember that it is his poetry which bears the

[3]This page and the following refer to the English translation of Bakhtin's *Toward a Philosophy of the Act*, ed. by M. Holquist and V. Liapunov, University of Texas Press, Austin, 1993.

> guilt for the vulgar prose of life, whereas the man of everyday life ought to know that the fruitlessness of art is due to his willingness to be unexacting and to the unseriousness of the concerns in his life. The individual must become answerable through and through: all of his constituent moments must not only fit next to each other in the temporal sequence of his life, but must also interpenetrate each other in the unity of guilt and answerability. [...] Art and life are not one, but they must become united in myself — in the unity of my answerability (Bakhtin 1919, Eng. trans.: 1-2).

On one hand, therefore, "special answerability", relative to a given domain of culture, a given content, a given role and function, delimited, defined, circumscribed answerability referred to the repeatable identity of the objective and interchangeable individual; on the other hand, "moral answerability", "absolute answerability", without limits, alibis, which alone renders individual action unique; answerability of the single individual that cannot be abdicated. The connection between these two kinds of answerability is that between objective, repetetive, identical meaning conferred by the domain of culture in which action is objectified, and the unrepeatable self-determination of being as a unique and unitary event, activity in its entirety and complexity though not decomposable or classifiable. Here Bakhtin anticipates the criteria used for the distinction between "theme" and "meaning", particularly important in his conception of the sign to which he dedicates an entire chapter in the volume of 1929 signed by Voloshinov.

The act of our activity, of actual experiencing, says Bakhtin, is therefore "a two-faced Janus" (p. 2) oriented in two different directions: never-repeatable uniqueness and objective, abstract unity. My answerable activity as a unique individual, wholly identified in a given moment and in given conditions is absolutely indifferent, "completely impervious" (p. 4) to the latter. The moment of unique event-ness in which judgment is an answerable act or deed of its author is absolutely *indifferent* to theoretical meaning, and therefore remains entirely outside thought as generally valid judgment. The theoretical veridicality of judgment does not explain how that judgment is the ought of thinking; vice versa the ought cannot ground the theoretical veridicality of judgment; the moment of theoretical veridicality is necessary but not sufficient for it to become an ought-to-be: this is why Bakhtin refuses Rickert's conception of *the ought* as the highest formal category, and citing Husserl affirms that the assumption of theoretically valid judgment as the ought cannot be derived from it, but rather can only be brought in from the outside. With respect to the ought, to the concrete act of its assumption, theoretical veridicality, says Bakhtin, only has a technical value. This is also true of all that is aesthetically, scientifically, morally significant: all such meanings have a technical value given that none contain ought in their content; this is to be traced instead in the unity of my unique answerable life as it is manifested in the uniqueness of answerable choice. The connection between objective, abstract, indifferent validity and the never-repeatable uniqueness of a standpoint, of a choice cannot be explained in terms of theoretical knowledge, thanks to an abstract theoretical subject, a gnoseological consciousness, precisely because all this has formal, technical validity indifferent to the answerable act of the single individual. Particularly important are Bakhtin's considerations on the autonomy of what is technologically valid, governed by its own immanent laws, acquiring a value of its own, power and dominion over the life of the single individual once it has lost its connection to the live uniqueness of answerable activity. "All that which is technological", says Bakhtin, "when divorced from the once occurent unity of life and surrendered to the will of the law immanent to its development, is frightening; it may from time to time irrupt into this once-occurent unity as an irresponsibly destructive and terrifying force (p. 7).

Bakhtin insists particularly on the alien character of the singularity of life as "answerable, risk-fraught, and open becoming" (p. 9) in the world of constructions by theoretical consciousness, its abstract *being* "lightened" of historical existence, determined as something unique and never-repeatable: absolute estrangement concerning the world as the object of knowledge in which everything finds a justification, except for the singularity of the existential position and of respective answering action. Insofar as by principle it is accomplished, finished, given, theoretical Being is *indifferent* to "that which is absolutely arbitrary (*answerably arbitrary*)" (p. 9), absolutely new and creative concerning unique life intended as continuous answerable activity; theoretical being "is indifferent to the central fact — central for me — of my unique and actual communion with Being" (p. 9) and of my "moral answerability", mine absolutely. And although the "unity-uniqueness" of my life-act remains alien to the indifferent theoretical consciousness, such unity-uniqueness is the foundation of the latter "insofar as the act of cognition as my deed is included, along with all its content, in the unity of its answerability, in which and by virtue of which I actually live — perform deeds" (p. 12). Therefore, says Bakhtin,

> Once-occurent uniqueness or singularity cannot be thought of, it can only be participatively experienced or lived through. All of theoretical reason in its entirety is only a moment of practical reason, i.e., the reason of the

unique *subiectum*'s moral orientation within the event of once-occurent Being (p. 13).

Bakhtin demonstrates the uselessness of attempts at recovering the unity-uniqueness of action-life whether through the forms of the reductionism of theoreticism, on the basis of which it is reconducted to the categories of a given cognitive field and thought in biological, psychological, sociological, economical terms, etc. (the reductionism of theoreticism, observes Bakhtin, is nothing less than "the inclusion of the large theoretical world within a small, also theoretical, world", p. 13); or through the philosophies of life and a certain tendency to aestheticize life, of which Bakhtin considers the most important to be the philosophy of Bergson. Bakhtin's critique of the Bergsonian notion of "intuition" —the notion of *empathy*, participative cognition, which in art is directed toward the individual, through which one enters the interiority of an object to coincide with what is unique in it— anticipates his critique of the concept of "empathy", designed to play a central role in the Bakhtinian conception of the otherness relationship from "Author and Hero" through to his writings of the 1970s. The concept of identification (which remains fundamentally theoretical, despite its aestheticism) leads to the illusive belief of being able to overcome the extraneousness, *"transgredient character"* (an expression present in Bakhtin's subsequent writings of the early 1920s and which plays a central role in the delineation of the concept of extralocality), uniqueness, otherness of the situation as from which the act of identification comes about: the concept of identification, as identification with the other involves, says Bakhtin, the loss of uniqueness of the unique place which I occupy in the world and presupposes, therefore, the assertion of the inessential character of my uniqueness and of the uniqueness of my place. Bakhtin makes a point of distinguishing between pure identification as a theoretical-aesthetic notion and "answerable act/deed of self-abstracting or self-renunciation" (p. 16). Pure empathizing is delusive for it cannot be achieved; if this were possible, it would involve the "impoverishment" of the relational situation, since "instead of two participants there would be one" (p. 16); and because of the discontinuance of my unique being and therefore as my not-being, it would also imply annulment of my consciousness rather than a cognitive modality. On the contrary, in self-sacrifice the uniqueness of one's being in the world is fully achieved and the world in which, from one's own unique place, the act of sacrifice of self is chosen responsibly, is not at all the indifferent world of theoretical consciousness and of aesthetic intuition. Therefore, aesthetic identification cannot enlighten us on the uniqueness of being in the world manifested when we take a stand, in answerable action. Rather, says Bakhtin,

> The entire aesthetic world as a whole is but a moment of Being-as-event through an answerable consciousness — through an answerable deed by a participant (p. 18).

If neither theoretical cognition nor the aesthetic grasp the unique event-ness of answerable action in the context of the uniqueness of being in the world, this is because they must both fundamentally abstract from the place occupied by the observer, from his uniqueness as interpreter, from his otherness and also from this uniqueness, never-repeatability-otherness of what is observed following its reduction to the status of object. Contemporary philosophy has drawn nearer and nearer to the ideal of scientificness, but because of this it has become a philosophy of the domains of culture and their specific unity, and always less able to account for unitary and unique Being-as-event in life-action. According to Bakhtin, this explains the attraction exerted through a contrast mechanism in the field of philosophy by the following two orientations, in spite of their shortcomings: by historical materialism with its aim of leaving the more abstract theoretical world to build a world with room for the performance of deeds that are determinate, concretely historical and as active and answerable as possible philosophical conceptions that, evoking the Middle Ages or Oriental philosophies, place the question of wisdom at the center of their interests. As much as they are different and opposite, Bakhtin evidences the common methodological limit to both these philosophical tendencies insofar as they fail to discriminate between "what is given and what is set as a task, what *is* and what *ought* to be" (p. 20).

Bakhtin's assertion that theoretical reason and aesthetic reason are both part of practical reason should not lead us to believe that he was a follower of Kantianism. Moral philosophy or "first philosophy", as he sometimes called it, which describes Being-as-event in terms of answerable action, cannot avail itself of the Kantian conception or of the Neo-Kantian revival even though they do consider the moral problem to be particularly important. Bakhtin accuses the formal ethics of Kant and the Kantians of theoreticism, that is, of "abstracting from my unique self": there is no approach to a living act performed in the real world (p. 27).

The philosophy of the answerable act, says Bakhtin, can only be the phenomenology, the participative description, of this world of action assumed not as contemplated or theoretically thought out from the outside, but rather from the inside in its answerability. Though connected with Husserl's phenomenology, the approach just described is substantially different given that it proposes the otherness relationship centerd on "moral answerability" as against the *noesis-noema*, subject-object relationship. From this point of view Bakhtin's attitude toward Husserl's phenomenology is similar to that adopted by Emmanuel Lévinas (cf. Ponzio 1992, 1994a, 1995b). The indifference of theoreticism is superseded by what is understood by the *unindifference* of participating in the world uniquely, never-repeatably and unreplaceably, by *"my non-alibi in being"*. As regards the condition of unindifference —which does not ensue from a theoretical admission, but which is the condition of my interest, desire, cognition, action, in which my uniqueness is simultaneously already given and actively set by myself, in which I am passive and active, determined and answerable—, we find that dogmatism and generic hypotheticism, absolute determinism and the abstract conception of freedom as void possibility, objectivism and all forms of subjectivism and psychologism, void rationalism —where logical clarity and abstract consequentiality are separated from answerable consciousness and act as obscure and uncontrolled forces—, and the irrationalism complementary to it, are all superseded: "rationality", says Bakhtin quoting Nietzsche, "is but a moment of answerability, a light that is 'like the glimmer of a lamp before the sun'" (p. 29). Language itself lives in relation to parti-cipative thought and action, and the word which is not an abstract word from the dictionary, nor subjectively casual, becomes a live and "answerably-significant" word in relation to them. We already have clearly expressed considerations on language in this early paper by Bakhtin which were to be developed in his subsequent books as well as in the two volumes by Voloshinov and in articles by the latter (cf. Voloshinov-Bakhtin 1980). It is in relation to the uniqueness of action that the word, says Bakhtin, manifests itself in its fullness, not only in terms of *content-sense*, but also as *expression-image* and, from an emotional-volitional viewpoint, as *intonation*. Unindifference deriving from the connection with answerable action orients words and makes possible the comprehension of objects, their living experience: to speak of an object means to enter an interested, unindifferent relationship with it, so that the uttered word cannot avoid being intonated. But all that is experienced is intonated and even the most abstract thought, insofar as it is concretely thought, has a volitional-emotional tone, and if an essential tie were not established between content and its emotional tone, which constitutes its actual value, a given word would not be uttered, a given thought would not be thought, a given object would not enter living experience.

In Bakhtin's view, the unindifference of answerable action establishes a connection between culture and life, between cultural consciousness and living consciousness. When this is not the case, cultural, cognitive, scientific, aesthetic, political values rise to the status of values-in-themselves and lose all possibility of verification, functionality, transformation. Bakhtin observes that this is part of a Hobbesian conception with clear political implications: to absolute cultural values there corresponds the conception according to which the people choose one time only, renouncing their freedom, surrendering themselves to the State after which they become slaves to their own free decision (cf. p. 35). In his subsequent research Bakhtin was to amply demonstrate how all this contradicts constitutive popular resistance to "State truth", the irreducibility of "non official ideology" to "official ideology", the character of popular culture whose capacity for innovation and regeneration in relation to dominant culture was to be the object of study in Bakhtin's monograph on Rabelais. Insofar as it belongs to "class ideology", at a certain point State truth, says Bakhtin in one of his subsequent annotations "From Notes Made in 1970-71", encounters the unsurmountable barrier of irony and degrading allegory, the carnivalesque spark of allegorical-ironical imprecation which destroys all gravity and seriousness and never dies in the heart of the people. In a passage from *Toward a Philosophy of the Act*, Bakhtin returns to the problem of the abdication of answerability, as political answerability, when he refers to political representation which in the attempt at relieving itself of political answerability often loses —both in whoever attributes it and in whoever assumes it— the sense of its roots in unique, personal non-alibi participation, and consequently becomes void, specialized and formal answerability, with all the danger that such loss of roots and of sense involves (cf. p. 52).

In *Toward a Philosophy of the Act*, Bakhtin refuses the concept of truth as inherited from rationalism, understood as formed of general, universal moments, as something that is repetetive and constant and as separate and set against the individual and the subjective. Vice versa, as says Bakhtin, the unity of real consciousness acting answerably must not be thought in terms of continuity, at the level of content, of principles, rights, the law, and even less so of being: this clearly being a critique of all forms of dogmatic absolutism, including the ontological. No being or value is identical or autonomous, a constant principle, separate from the live action of its identification as that given being or value.

As regards the critique of ontology (extensible to Heidegger's ontology) as an important moment in the Bakhtinian refounding of "first philosophy" as "moral philosophy", the following passage from *Toward a Philosophy of the Act* is particularly significant:

> Participation in the being-event of the world in its entirety does not coincide, from our point of view, with irresponsible self-surrender to Being, with being-possessed by Being. What happens in the latter case is that the passive moment in my participation is moved to the fore, while my to-be-accomplished self-activity is reduced. The aspiration of Nietzsche's philosophy is reduced to a considerable extent to this possessedness by Being (one-sided participation); its ultimate result is the absurdity of contemporary Dionysianism (p. 49).

My "non-alibi in being" implies my uniqueness and irreplaceability, it transforms void possibility into answerable real action, it confers actual validity and sense to all meanings and values which would otherwise be abstract, "it gives a face" to the event which is otherwise anonymous, it causes neither objective nor subjective reason to exist, but each one of us to be right in his/her own place and to be right not subjectively but answerably, without the possibility of interpretation as a "contradiction" if not for a third, disembodied, non-participating consciousness and in the perspective of abstract, non-dialogic dialectics, which Bakhtin was to explicitly call into question in "From Notes Made in 1970-71". "Non-alibi in being" relates the I to the other, in a relation that in not an indifferent relation with a generic other (both terms, the I and the others, being examples of man in general) but in a relation of concrete involvement, unindifference with the life of one's neighbour, one's contemporary, with the past and future of real persons. An abstract truth referred to man in general, such as "man is mortal", acquires sense and value, says Bakhtin, only from my unique place, as the death of my neighbour, my own death, as the death of an entire community, or as the possibility of elimination of the whole of historically real humanity:

> And, of course, the emotional-volitional, valuative sense of my death, of the death of an other who is dear to me, and the fact of any actual person's death are all profoundly different in each case, for all these are different moments in once-occurent Being-as-event. For a disembodied, detached (non-participating) *subiectum*, all deaths may be equal. No one, however, lives in a world in which all human beings are —with respect to value— equally mortal (p. 48).

Bakhtin insists particularly on the inevitability of involvement with the other —with the concrete other, and not with an abstract other self, theoretistically conceived as abstract gnoseological consciousness— implied by the condition of answerable participation in the world from the uniqueness of one's place: to be answerably participative is also apprehension for the other, who compels me answerably;

answerability of the deed is above all answerability for the other, and my uniqueness is the impossibility to abdicate such answerability, not being replaceable in it, to the point of abnegation, of self-sacrifice which my "answerable centrality" alone makes possible, thereby becoming "sacrificed centrality".

One may also attempt to escape from this kind of non-alibi answerability, but even attempts at unburdening oneself testify to its weight and inevitable presence. All determinate roles, with their determinate, special answerability, do not abolish but simply specialize my personal answerability, says Bakhtin, that is, my moral answerability without limits or guarantees, without an alibi. Detached from absolute answerability, special answerability loses sense, becomes casual, technical answerability, and having become mere representation of a role, action, technical performance, as "technical activity" it is de-realized and becomes illusion.

Bakhtin characterizes contemporary crisis as the crisis of contemporary action which has become technical action; he identifies this crisis in the separation of action, with its concrete motivation, from its product, which consequently is emptied of sense. This interpretation is similar to Husserl's phenomenology, particularly as developed in *Die Krisis der europäischen Wissenschaften und die transzendentale Phänomenologie* (published posthumously in 1954). But in Bakhtin, differently from Husserl where a certain theoreticism persists, sense is not conferred by the intentional consciousness, by the transcendental subject, but by answerable action as expressed by the uniquess of non-alibi in being in the world. For Bakhtin a philosophy of life can only be a moral philosophy. Furthermore, Bakhtin emphasizes how separation of the product from the answerable act, of the technological-scientific apparatus from concrete motivation, of culture from life, not only implies to weaken the product, a loss of sense in the cultural world become autonomous dominion, knowledge emptied of sense, but also degradation of the act itself, which isolated from the meanings of culture, impoverished of its ideal aspects, descends to a low degree of biological and economic motivation: outside objective culture, the act appears as mere biological subjectivity, an act-need. On considering this aspect, Bakhtin refers explicitly to Spengler, underlining his inability to reconduct theory and thought to action as parts of action, instead of opposing them to action. This is possible once action is considered as unitary and unique answerable action distinct from technical action with its special answerability (cf. p. 56).

Moral philosophy must describe the "concrete architectonics" of the actual world of the performed act as a unitary and once-occurent act or deed, the basic emotional-volitional aspects of the latter's construction and their mutual arrangement. The aspects of such architectonics in the light of which all values, meanings and spatial-temporal relationships are constituted and arranged are characterized by Bakhtin in terms of otherness. They are: "I-for-myself, the other-for-me, and I-for-the-other" (p. 54).

> All the values of actual life and culture are arranged around the basic architectonic points of the actual world of the performed act or deed: scientific values; aesthetic values; political values (including both ethical and social values); and, finally, religious values (p. 54).

In the part entitled "I" following the introduction to *Toward a Philosophy of the Act*, Bakhtin, starting from the unique place which each one of us occupies irreplaceably, concretely deals with the architectonics of the uniqueness and volitional-emotional unity of the world, considered as a non systematic but concretely-architectonic whole, from an axiological and spatial-temporal viewpoint: such a unity is arranged around a unique participative and unindifferent center, the center of value represented by each one of us in our non-alibi answerability. This kind of architectonics could not be understood if actualized by the same subject around which it is organized, if belonging to the same self and therefore to the discourse of the "confession" genre or of any other genre of direct discourse which as such is incapable of developing a global vision. Nor is comprehension possible from a cognitive viewpoint which is neither emotionally nor evaluatively participative; which from an objective, indifferent point of view is incapable of *comprehending* what it describes and which would therefore end up impoverishing the latter and losing sight of the details which render it living and unfinalizable. Nor can it be based on empathy which would also be an impoverishment, if this were possible, insofar as it would reduce the relationship between two mutually external and non interchangeable positions to a single vision. According to Bakhtin, interpretation-comprehension architectonics presupposes the other, both different and unindifferent, but reciprocally participative. Consequently, there are two value-centers, myself and the other, the two value-centers of life itself around which the architectonics of answerable action is organized and arranged. And these two centers of value must remain reciprocally other, the architectonic relationship between two others must remain from a spatial-temporal and axiological viewpoint, and the viewpoint of the I must not dominate. As an example of such a vision Bakhtin analyses the architectonics of art in *Toward a Philosophy of the Act*, specifically verbal art, literature, which is organized around the center of value represented by the single human being in its uniqueness, irreplaceability, precariousness and mortality. With respect to the latter, such expressions as earlier, later, as yet, when, never, late, already, it's necessary, ought to, beyond, farther, nearer, lose their abstract meaning, says Bakhtin, and are charged each time with a concrete sense relative to the emotional-volitional situation of this participative center. Bakhtin develops and specifies such statements in "Author and Hero in Aesthetic Activity":

> My own axiological relationship to myself is completely unproductive aesthetically: for myself, I am aesthetically unreal. [...]. The organizing power in all aesthetic forms is the axiological category of the *other*, the relationship to the other, enriched by an axiological "excess" of seeing for the purpose of achieving a transgredient consummation (Bakhtin 1920-23, Eng. trans.: 188-189).

Bakhtin finds that the architectonics he intends to analyse with his moral philosophy or first philosophy is ready in literature: literary writing installs a relationship that maintains the otherness of the center of value of this architectonics, considered from a transgredient, extralocalized point of view, in turn unique and other. This is the author/hero relationship in the sphere of the literary text.

Every part of an artwork may be considered as a reaction of the author to a reaction of the hero toward an object, an event: *reaction to a reaction*. The relationship of the author, of art, to life is indirect, mediated by the hero. In life too we encounter situations formed of reactions to reactions: but here the human reacted to as well as his reaction are assumed in their objectivity, and the reaction to the reaction is also objective, it expresses a standpoint and is functional to a given context, a given aim. On the contrary, on an artistic plane the hero's reaction is represented and is no longer objective, but objectified, distanced from the author-man, it is his own reaction. The distinction between "objective" and "objectified" as well as the related distinction between "author man" and "author creator" play an important role in Bakhtin's conception and can, in fact, be traced throughout the whole course of his production, from his early writings of the 1920s to his later writings of the 1970s. The reaction to life, to the hero, is neither provisional nor functional to a practical or cognitive end insofar as it is objectified. A unitary reaction to the totality of the hero's world is essential to the artwork. This reaction is distinct from cognitive and practical reactions, though it is not indifferent to them; it gathers all the single cognitive and emotional-volitional reactions and unites them into an architectonic whole. For it to assume artistic value, the author's unitary action must evidence the resistance of reality, of life, which finds expression in the hero, the resistance of what is objective with respect to its rendering, to its objectification; the author's unitary action must evidence the hero's otherness and his extra-artistic values, it must therefore begin from a position of extralocality —in space, time and sense— as regards the hero, specially if autobiographical. Differently, as in the case of autobiography, the author's unitary action assumes confessional tones devoid of artistic value. In all this we clearly find traces of Bakhtin's critique of Russian Formalism which was to be systematically developed in *The Formal Method in Literary Scholar-ship*, 1928, signed by Medvedev.

In the part marked "I" ("First") of *Toward a Philosophy of the Act*, Bakhtin analyses a poem by Pushkin, *Razluka* (*Parting*) in his effort to clarify the architectonic layout of the aesthetic vision. Subsequently, he was to focus on the relationship between "author and hero in aesthetic activity" producing a long paper with the same title in which the first chapter, as mentioned above, begins with an analysis of the same poem, developing considerations which had already been made in the final part of the fragment now at our disposal. This is particularly interesting to the end of understanding the direction of Bakhtin's research. We shall not stop now to examine this part (but refer the reader to our comment in the Italian edition of "Fragment from the first chapter of 'Author and Hero'", cf. Ponzio-Jachia 1993). Here we shall simply say that Bakhtin identified the type of architectonics he wished to analyse in the viewpoint of literature. However, what was intended as an example ended up holding his attention for the rest of his life so that the viewpoint of literature became his main focus.

Another important point is that Bakhtin initially approached the aesthetic vision through the lyrical genre, in which he had originally identified the relationship of dialogic otherness among different points of view — in the case of Pushkin's poetry, the dialogic dialectic between the author's context and that of the two protagonists, between the author-hero and the heroine. All this contradicts both the mistaken interpretation that Bakhtin did not sufficiently consider the lyrical genre; as well as the misunderstanding about his conception of dialogicality; for Bakhtin dialogicality is a question of *degree*. Contrary to those critics who have wrongly interpreted Bakhtin as having perspected a rigid opposition between absolutely monological genres, e.g. lyric poetry, and dialogical genres, specially the "polyphonic" novel (as identified in the works of Dostoevsky), for Bakhtin dialogicality is always present in the artistic word to varying degrees and as such it characterizes the different genres.

Furthermore, his belief that "first philosophy" or "moral philosophy" (whose foundations he critically analyses) is centered on the uniqueness and irreducible otherness of being, requiring not a direct, objective vision of the "I", of the subject, but an indirect and objectified vision where the viewpoint of "other" (as developed in literary writing) is central, gives us an insight into what he means by "metalinguistics" (as this term is used in *Dosteovsky*): the living dynamic reality of language cannot be understood by studying the direct word, nor by linguistics when it abstracts from the internal dialogicality of the concretely oriented and specifically intonated word. *Toward a Philosophy of the Act* states the premisses that were to guide Bakhtin throughout the whole course of his research. As he demonstrated in a paper of 1952-53, "The Problem of Speech Genres", discourse genres may be divided into *primary* or *simple genres,* the genres of everyday dialogue, and *secondary* or *complex* genres, the literary genres which instead render and objectify everyday, ordinary, objective dialogical exchange. As a component of secondary genres, dialogue in primary genres is pictured so that it loses its immediate connection with the real context and with the aims of everyday life and, therefore, its instrumentality and functionality. The word *leaves its monological context* in which it is determined in relation to its object and the other words forming its context, and enters the context of the word that pictures it. This is the complex context of verbal interaction with the author who objectifies and renders the direct word in the form of indirect, direct and free indirect discourse and their variants (discussed in part three of *Marxism and the Philosophy of Language,* Voloshinov-Bakhtin, 1929, now available in a new Italian edition translated directly from Russian, cf. Voloshinov-Bakhtin 1999). Bakhtin maintains that the complexity of dialogue may be studied through the pictured word and its internal dialogization, found in the secondary discourse genres of literature —specially the novel— which evidence aspects of dialogue that do not emerge in primary, simple, direct, objective discourse genres. Such a study is particularly interesting, as Bakhtin 1952-53 maintains, when the object of analysis is the *utterance* considered as the *cell of dialogic exchange,* and not the *sentence* or *proposition,* the utterance as the cell of *the system of language.* (The latter is an abstract concept reviewed by Bakhtin in the light of his critique of "abstract objectivism" in language studies; on these aspects see Voloshinov's 1929 volume as well as his 1928 paper on tendencies in linguistic studies, It. trans. in Voloshinov-Bakhtin 1980).

> A one-sided orientation toward primary genres inevitably leads to a vulgarization of the entire problem (behaviorist linguistics is an extreme example). The very interrelations between primary and secondary genres and the process of the historical formation of the latter shed light on the nature of the utterance (and above all on the complex problem of the in-

terrelations among language, ideology, and world view) (Bakhtin 1952-53, Eng. trans.: 62).

Bakhtin's text on the philosophy of the answerable act sheds light on the itinerary which led him to his 1929 monograph on Dostoevsky. According to Bakhtin, Dostoevsky's "philosophy" must not be identified with the specific conceptions and standpoints of the heroes in his novels or with specific contents. On the contrary, Bakhtin finds traces of the architectonics theorized in his paper on moral philosophy in the overall structure of Dostoevsky's works, which he describes as organized according to the principle of dialogicality. This is what Bakhtin was alluding to when he says, "to affirm someone else's 'I' not as an object but as another subject — this is the principle governing Dostoevsky's worldview" (Bakhtin 1963, Eng. trans.: 11): a statement which also becomes clearer in the light of a paper of 1914 on Dostoevsky by Vjačeslav Ivanov (1973). In Dostoevsky's "polyphonic novel" the character is no longer described by an "I" and assumed as an object. On the contrary, the character itself is a center of otherness and organizes its world from this perspective:

> Not without reason does Dostoevsky force Makar Devushkin to read Gogol's "Overcoat" and to take it as a story about himself [...] Dostoevsky carried out, as it were, a small-scale Copernican revolution when he took what had been a firm and finalizing authorial definition and turned it into an aspect of the hero's self-definition. [...]
>
> Devushkin had glimpsed himself in the image of the hero of "The Overcoat," which is to say, as something totally quantified, measured, and defined to the last detail: all of you is here, there is nothing more in you, and nothing more to be said about you. He felt himself to be hopelessly predetermined and finished off, as if he were already quite dead, yet at the same time he sensed the falseness of such an approach. [...]
>
> The serious and deeper meaning of this revolt might be expressed this way: a living human being cannot be turned into the voiceless object of some secondhand, finalizing cognitive process. *In a human being there is always something that only he himself can reveal; in a free act of self-consciousness and discourse; something that does not submit to an externalizing secondhand definition.* [...]
>
> The genuine life of the personality is made available only through a dialogic penetration of that personality, during which it freely and reciprocally reveals itself (Bakhtin 1963, Eng. trans.: 49-59).

This is the direction of Bakhtin's research from his early writings to his 1929 monograph on Dostoevsky: on delineating the principles of his prolegomena to a philosophy of responsible action for the reformulation of philosophy, he discovered the possibility of their full expression in literary writing. Such a possibility is determined by the fact that literary writing is able to transcend the dimension of identity and the limits of the difference-indifference relation, to varying degrees, depending on the literary genres or subgenres in question, and, therefore, to delineate the architectonics of otherness in a perspective that is participative and unindifferent. Such an orientation is also present throughout the research of the members of the Bakhtin Circle (as evidenced, for example, by the collection of writings published in *Bachtin e le sue maschere,* cf. Bakhtin *et alii* 1995). On the basis of this initial interest in the philosophy of responsible action, Bakhtin develops an interest in the philosophy of literature, where *of literature* is a subject genetive: the philosophical worldview which literature, verbal art, makes possible, and not a philosophical view to which literature must be subjected.

Surprisingly, Bakhtin's most recent paper, of 1974, "Toward a Methodology for the Human Sciences" (in Bakhtin 1979, Eng. trans.: 159-172) insists on the same question, proposed from the very beginning of his research. This paper, which was written on the basis of materials developed by Bakhtin toward the end of the 1930s or beginning of the 1940s, returns to the problem of the impossibility of applying categories proper to the subject-object relationship to the human world. When dealing with human expression the criterion is neither the "exactness" of knowledge, nor philosophical "rigour", in the Husserlian sense, but the "profoundness of answering comprehension".

Most interesting is the fact that at the beginning of this paper, after describing dialogic-active comprehension as the highest level of sign comprehension, Bakhtin should refer to the "symbol" recalling an encyclopedic entry by S. S. Averinčev ("Sinvol", in *Kratkaja literaturnaja enciclopedija,* vol. VI, Moskva 1971), who collaborated with Bakhtin in addition to editing his writings. Using Averinčev's conceptualization of "artistic symbol", Bakhtin focuses on the connection to the image upon which the symbol "confers *depth* and sense perspective" (cf. Bakhtin 1979, It. trans.: 375). The symbol implies a "dialectic correlation between identity and non-identity". In the symbol, adds Bakhtin citing Averinčev, "there is 'the warmth of a mystery that unites', juxtaposition of one's *own* to the *other,* the warmth of love and the chill of extraneousness. Juxtaposition and confrontation" (cf. *ibidem*). Bakhtin insists that sense in the symbol-image requires relatedness to another sense and interpretation not on the basis of its closest context, but rather of a remote context, a distant context, which opens identity to alterity. It is clear that such considerations are closely connected to those made by Bakhtin in his text on the philosophy of responsible action.

In an essay entitled "Allegoria e metodo della conoscenza in Bachtin and in Benjamin. Due note e una parenesi" (in Ponzio-Jachia 1993: 43-56), Romano Luperini underlines a possible connection between the Bakhtinian concept of symbol and Ricoeur's, maintaining that it may be associated to the notion of "allegory" as understood by both Bakhtin himself as well as by Walter Benjamin. Particularly interesting is the fact that Luperini evidences the essential features of the Bakhtinian conception of interpretation beginning from the concept of "symbol" as analysed by Bakhtin in his 1974 paper, but which, as we have shown, had already been clearly delineated in *Toward a Philosophy of the Act*. These features include: Bakhtin's surpassing of traditional approaches of the subjectivistic and idealistic type, and of the objectivistic and scientistic type; his critique of positivistic, neopositivistic, and historicist positions as well as of dogmatic Marxism; his refusal of reducing interpretation to a simple encounter between two consciousnesses, to a "fusion of horizons" *à la* Gadamer, which annuls distance and mutual extralocality among texts in the historical *continuum* and in the linearity of tradition.

References

Averinčev, S. S.

1971 "Sinvol", in *Kratkaja literaturnaja enciclopedija*, vol. VI, Moscow, coll. 826-831; It. trans. in Ponzio-Jachia 1993, pp. 197-207.

Averinčev, S. S.; Bocharov, S.

1979 "Note al testo", in M. Bakhtin 1979, It. trans. 1988.

Bakhtin, Mikhail M.

1919 "Art and Answerability (1919)", in Bakhtin 1979, Eng. trans. 1990, pp. 1-3; It. trans. in Bakhtin *et alii* 1995, pp. 41-42.

1920-23 "Author and Hero in Aesthetic Activity", in Bakhtin 1979, Eng.trans. 1990, pp. 4-256.

1922a *Toward a Philosophy of the Act*, ed. by M. Holquist & V. Liapunov (trans.), University of Texas Press, Austin, 1993; It. trans. "Per una filosofia dell'azione responsabile", in Bakhtin 1995 et alii, pp. 43-100; see also Bakhtin 1998.

1922b "L'autore e l'eroe nell'attività estetica. Frammento del capitolo primo", posthumously ed. by S. Bocharov in *Filosofija i sočiologija nauki i tekniki: Ezegodnik 1984-1985*, Nauka, Moscow 1986, It. trans. in Ponzio-Jachia 1993, pp. 159-184.

1922c "L'autore e l'eroe nell'attività estetica" (capitolo secondo), ed. posthumously by S. Averinčev and S. Bocharov, in M. Bachtin 1979, It. trans. 1988b, pp. 5-187.

1924 "Il problema del contenuto, del materiale e della forma nella creazione letteraria", in M. Bachtin 1975, It. trans. 1979, pp. 3-66.

1929a *Problemy tvorčestva Dostoevskogo,* Leningrad, Priboj, It. trans. *Problemi dell'opera di Dostoevsky,* trans. & intro. by M. De Michiel, pres. by A. Ponzio, Edizioni dal Sud, Bari, 1997.

1929b "Dal libro *Problemi dell' opera di Dostoevskij,* 1929", in M. Bachtin 1979, It. trans. 1988.

1934-35 "Discourse in the Novel", in Bakhtin 1975, Eng. trans. 1981, pp. 259-422.

1938 "Epic and the Novel", in Bakhtin 1975, Eng. trans. 1981, pp. 3-40.

1952-53 "The Problem of Speech Genres", in Bakhtin 1979, Eng. trans. 1986, pp. 60-102.

1959-61 "The Problem of the Text in Linguistics, Philology, and the Human Sciences: An Experiment in Philosophical Analysis", in Bakhtin 1975, Eng. trans. 1986, pp. 103-131.

1961"Toward a Reworking of the Dostoevsky Book", in Bakhtin 1979; Eng. trans. in Bakhtin, *Problems of Dostoevsky's Poetics (1929),* by C. Emerson (ed.), University of Minnesota Press, Minneapolis, Minn., 1984, pp. 283-302.

1963 *Problemy poetiki Dostoevskogo,* Moscow, Sovetskij pisatel'; Eng. trans *Problems of Dostoevsky's Poetics (1929),* by C. Emerson (ed.), University of Minnesota Press, Minneapolis, Minn., 1984.

1965 *Tvorčestvo Fransua Rable i narodnaja kul'tura srednevekov'ja i,* Moscow; Eng. trans. *Rabelais and His World,* by H. Iswolsky, Indiana University Press, Bloomington, Indiana, 1984.

1970-71 "From Notes Made in 1970-71", in Bakhtin 1979, Eng. trans. 1986, pp. 132-158.

1971 "Sulla polifonicità dei romanzi di Dostoevskij", It. trans. in M. Bachtin, *Tolstoj* (testi 1922- 1971), ed. by V. Strada, Il Mulino, Bologna, 1986, pp. 131-141.

1974 "Toward a Methodology for the Human Sciences", in Bakhtin 1979, Eng. trans. 1986, pp. 159-172.

1975 *Voprosy literatury i estetiki* (Problems of Literature and of Aesthetics), Chudozestvennaja literatura, Moscow; It. trans. *Estetica e romanzo,* Einaudi, Turin,1979.

1979 *Estetika slovesnogo tvorčestva* (Aesthetics of verbal art), Iskusstvo, Moscow, 1979; It. trans. *L'autore e l'eroe. Teoria letteraria e scienze umana,* Einaudi, Turin, 1988.

1981 *The Dialogic Imagination. Four Essays,* ed. by M; Holquist, trans. by C. Emerson and M. Holquist, University of Texas Press, Austin, 1981.

1986 *Speech Genres & Other Late Essays*, trans. by V. McGee, ed. by C. Emerson and M. Holquist, University of Texas Press, Austin.

1990 *Art and Answerability. Early Philosophical Essays by M.M. Bakhtin*, ed. by M. Holquist and V. Liapunov, trans. and notes by V. Liapunov, suppl. trans. by K. Brostrom, University of Texas Press, Austin, 1990.

1993 *Toward a Philosophy of the Act*, trans. and notes by V. Liapunov, ed. by M. Holquist & V. Liapunov, University of Texas Press, Austin; It. trans. in Bakhtin *et alii* 1995, pp. pp. 43-100; new revised etition Bakhtin 1998.

1997 *Hacia una filosofía del acto ético. De los borradores y otros escritos*, Comentarios de Iris M. Zavala y Augusto Ponzio, trad. del ruso de T. Bubnova, Anthropos, Barcelona; Editorial de la Universidad de Puerto Rico, San Juan.

1998 *Per una filosofia dell'azione responsabile*, con due saggi di Augusto Ponzio e Iris M. Zavala, trans. from 2nd Russian ed. by M. De Michiel, Piero Manni, Lecce.

Bakhtin, M. M.; Kanaev, I. I.; Medvedev, P. N.; Voloshinov, V. N.

1995 *Bachtin e le sue maschere. Il percorso bachtiniano fino ai Problemi dell'opera di Dostoevskij (1919-1929)*, ed. by A. Ponzio & P. Jachia, M. De Michiel, Dedalo, Bari.

Benjamin, Walter

1963 *Ursprung des deutschen Trauerspiels*, Suhrkamp, Verlag, Frankfurt am Main; It. trans. *Il dramma barocco tedesco*, Einaudi, Turin, 1971.

Husserl, Edmund

1954 *Die Krisis der europäischen Wissenschaften und die transzendentale Phänomenologie*, ed. by W. Biemel, Husserliana, Band VI, Matinus Nijoff, Den Haag 1959.

Ivanov, Vjaceslav V.

1973 "Significato delle idee di Bachtin sul segno, l'atto di parola e il dialogo per la semiotica contemporanea", It. trans. in V.V. Ivanov, J. Kristeva et al., *Michail Bachtin. Semiotica, teoria della letteratura e marxismo*, ed. by A. Ponzio, Dedalo, Bari, 1977, pp. 67-104.

Jachia, Paolo

1992 *Introduzione a Bachtin*, Laterza, Bari.

1993a "Il fondamento metalinguistico della filosofia critica e dialogica di M. Bachtln", *Strumenti Critici*, 3.

1993b Bachtin e gli altri 'autori' delle sue opere: il Circolo di Bachtin e il marxismo", in Ponzio-Jachia 1993, pp. 5-24.

Kanaev, I. I.

1926 " Il vitalismo contemporaneo", It. trans. in Bakhtin *et alii* 1995, pp. 175-198.

Luperini, Romano

1993 "Allegoria e metodo della conoscenza in Bachtin and in Benjamin. Due note e una parenesi", in Ponzio-Jachia 1993, pp. 43-56.

Medvedev, Pavel N.

1928 *Formal'nyj metod v literaturovedenii*, Leningrad; It. trans. *Il metodo formale nella scienza della letteratura* , Dedalo, Bari, 1978; Eng. trans. *The Formal Method In Literary Scholarship: A Critical Introduction to Sociological Poetics*, Eng. trans. by A.J. Wehrle, The Johns Hopkins University Press, Baltimore, 1978.

Ponzio, Augusto

1980 *Michail Bachtin. Alle origini della semiotica sovietica,* Dedalo, Bari.

1981 *Segni e contraddizioni. Tra Marx e Bachtin,* Bertani, Verona.

1991 *Dialogo e narrazione*, Milella, Lecce.

1992 *Tra semiotica e letteratura. Introduzione a Michail Bachtin,* Bompiani, Milan.

1993 "Nota" alla traduzione it. di Bachtin 1922b.

1994a *Scrittura dialogo e alterità. Tra Bachtin e Lévinas* , La Nuova Italia, Florence.

1994b *Fondamenti di filosofia del linguaggio* (in collab. with P. Calefato & S. Petrilli), Laterza, Bari, new ed. 1999.

1995a *La differenza non indifferente. Comunicazione, migrazione, guerra,* Mimesis, Milan.

1995b *Responsabilità e alterità in Emmanuel Lévinas,* Jaca Book, Milan.

1996 *Sujet et altérité. Sur Emmanuel Lévinas,* suivi de Deux dialogues avec Emmanuel Lévinas, L'Harmattan, Paris.

1997a *La rivoluzione bachtiniana. Il pensiero di Bachtin e l'ideologia contemporanea,* Levante Editore, Bari; Spanish edition, *La revolución Bajtiniana. El pensamiento de Bajtín y la ideología contemporánea,* trans. by M. Arriaga, Frónesis Cátedra, Univesitat de València, Madrid, 1998.

1997b "Para una filosofia de la acción", in M. M. Bakhtin 1997, pp. 225-246.

Ponzio, Augusto; Jachia, Paolo

1993 (ed.) *Bachtin e...* , Laterza, Bari.

Rolland, Jacques

1990 *Dostoevskij e la questione dell'altro,* Jaca Book, Milan.

Titunik, I. R.

1973 "Metodo formale e metodo storico", in V.V. Ivanov, J. Kristeva et al., *Michail Bachtin. Semiotica, teoria della letteratura e marxismo* , ed. by A. Ponzio, Dedalo, Bari, 1977, pp. 161-198.

Voloshinov, Valentin N.; Bakhtin, Mikhail M.

1926 "Discourse in Life and Discourse in Poetry: Questions of Sociological Poetics", Eng. trans. by J. Richmond, in *Bakhtin School Papers*, ed. by A. Shukman, RPT Publications in association with Dept. of Lit., Univ. of Essex, Colchester, Somerton, Oxford, 1988, pp. 5-30.

1927 *Frejdizm*, Moscow-Leningrad; It. trans. *Freudismo*, Bari, Dedalo, 1977; Eng. trans. *Freudianism: A Critical Sketch*, trans. by I.R. Titunik, ed. by I.R.Titunik with N.H.Bruss, Indiana University Press, Indianapolis, Ind., 1987.

1928 "Le più recenti tendenze del pensiero linguistico occidentale", It. trans. in Voloshinov-Bakhtin 1980, pp. 165-200.

1929 *Marksizm i filosofija jazyca*, Leningrad; Eng. trans. *Marxism and the Philosophy of Language*, by L. Matejka and I.R. Titunik, Harvard University Press, Cambridge, Mass., 1973; It. trans. from the English, *Marxismo e filosofia del linguaggio*, Bari, Dedalo, 1976; but see also Voloshinov-Bakhtin 1999.

1980 *Il linguaggio come pratica sociale* (saggi 1926-30), ed. by A. Ponzio, Dedalo, Bari.

Voloshinov, Valentin;

1999 *Marxismo e filosofia del linguaggio*, ed. & pres. by A. Ponzio, trans. from Russian and intro. by M. De Michiel, Piero Manni, Lecce.

Susan Petrilli

Bakhtinian Categories of Literature for a New Approach to Philosophy of Language

The aim of this paper is to show how fundamental categories in the philosophy of language may be renewed and improved in the light of Mikhail M. Bakhtin's (1895-1975) theory of literature. Through application of the category of otherness, which is central to Bakhtin's theory of literary writing, such concepts as sign, utterance, text, discourse genre and linguistic creativity may at last be redefined. Bakhtin's focus on dialogicality and literature shifts the study of language in the direction of what he calls "metalinguistics" in his book of 1929 on Dostoevsky, and "philosophy of language" in another book of 1929 (co-authored with Valentin N. Voloshinov) as well as in a later essay, "The Problem of the Text in Linguistics, Philology, and the Human Sciences", of 1959-1961.

On one hand, Bakhtin's theory of literary language reveals the limits of conceptions of language offered by the sciences of language; on the other, it renews the study of verbal signs through the categories of *dialogue* and *otherness*. On the basis of Bakhtinian theory it is possible to develop new theoretical horizons in the philosophy of language which, through the perspective of literature, reconsider and redefine such concepts as those mentioned above, sign, utterance, text, discourse genre and linguistic creativity, freeing them from their connections with the category of identity and associating them instead to the category of otherness.

Bakhtin and his Circle (as represented, for example, by *Marxism and the Philosophy of Language*, (cf. Bakhtin-Voloshinov 1929) contribute significantly to developments in philosophy of language which do not focus exclusively on verbal language nor limit themselves to confrontation with linguistics and its various approaches. On the contrary, Bakhtin analyzes the sign in its different manifestations of both the verbal and nonverbal order, thereby opening to confrontation with general semiotics. *Marxism and the Philosophy of Language* offers a critique of Saussurean linguistics as formulated in *Cours di linguistique général* (1916) and of the sign conception at its basis, as well as of the behaviourist conception of communication. Furthermore, in *Rabelais and His World* (1965) Bakhtin makes a thorough study of nonverbal language with special reference to the signs of carnival and their translation into verbal language, and of the processes of renewal and regeneration that such translation and carnivalization of literature involve for the literary word.

However, our focus in the present paper is not directed to Bakhtin's reflections (and those of his school) on verbal and nonverbal language, but rather to the contribution that may come from Bakhtin as a literary scholar to philosophy of language. In particular, we wish to evidence Bakhtin's treatment of the literary text which he never considers separately from the global network of verbal and nonverbal signs. Such interrelatedness of the literary text with all other signs forming the great sign network contributes to explaining its semiotical consistency and resistance, that is, its alterity and, therefore, its capacity for dialogic reaction with respect to its interpretations.

This orientation is a distinguishing feature of Bakhtin's research. Although he dedicated a large part of his research to theory of literature and literary criticism, he broke the boundaries not only of those disciplines that were directly concerned with literature, but also of those concerned with art in general. Bakhtin was intent upon demonstrating that a literary text can only be adequately understood by shifting one's gaze beyond literature and art generally, to view that text from different disciplinary perspectives, according to a process of extralocalization. For example, studies on verbal and nonverbal signs come into play, both at a theoretical level —that of general semiotics— and at the level of the specification of these studies relatively to different cultural systems, folklore traditions, festivities, rites, myths, and cults. In addition to verbal and nonverbal signs, other perspectives that come into play in the study of the literary text include the study of ideology, when analyzing the psychological and psychoanalytical relation between consciousness and the unconscious, the problem of social stratification and of the relation among social classes, the relation between history and structure, and between the genetic and the morphological approach, etc. Such a method inevitably involves all the human sciences, although Bakhtin never abandoned his special interest, that is, the problem of the specificity of the *literary* word. In a volume written with Pavel N. Medvedev and signed by the latter, *The Formal Method in Literary Scholarship* (1928), Bakhtin uses the ability to deal with the problem of the specificity of the literary word as a criterion for criticizing the Russian Formalists (who thought they had solved this problem), as well as those who thought they could get rid of the issue with superficial sociological formulae and pseudo-marxist slogans.

Bakhtin dealt with issues connected with literary writing from the viewpoint of literature itself. His excursions outside the field of literature did not imply recourse to an external viewpoint with claims to offering a totalizing and systemic description. On the contrary, Bakhtin remained inside literature and never left it; literature was his observatory, and it was from this perspective that he conducted his anti-systemic and detotalizing critique, revealing the internal threads which connect the literary to the extra-literary and underlining, therefore, the structural intertextuality subtending the connection among literary and extra-literary texts. In Bakhtin's view, the literary text subsists and develops in its specificity *as a literary text* thanks to its implication with the external universe, which is also of the ethical order.

Consequently, although literature was one of his main interests, it was not the only one. And not only did he focus his attention on the relation between "literature" and "life" (a central issue in his 1928 book), or more extensively between "art" and "life" (his earliest paper "Art and Answerability", 1919, clearly testifies to this, cf. Bakhtin 1979, English trans: 1-3), but also on the human sciences in general as emerges from the whole course of his production.

Bakhtin's multiple interests as far as the human sciences were concerned, and especially his research method, ultimately refer to the problem of value. From what we have said so far we could conclude that he was directly interested in the problem of aesthetic value with a particular interest for literary value, but given that he identified artistic value in otherness and extralocality, he necessarily dealt with other kinds of value as well.

These include, in the first place, ethical value. And, in fact, Bakhtin had already highlighted the importance of the connection between art and answerability in his 1919 paper, which include these two terms in the title. If, as he maintains in a paper of 1920-23, "Author and Hero in Aesthetic Activity", the source of artistic value is the category of other and not I, aesthetic value necessarily involves questions of an ethical order centering on the problem of the other. From this point of view, literature represents a sort of experiment, pushed to the extreme (beyond the limits of social convention), on the way values function in interpersonal relationships.

But this involves experimentation relatively to the dialogic character of the word as well. In literature, especially in certain genres such as the novel, the word's dialogicality may be examined beyond its limited reach in ordinary language. In Bakhtin, aesthetic value is reconnected to linguistic value as well as to human value, value as it characterizes the human person, considered not only in terms of identity but also of otherness. In Bakhtin's description, linguistic value is far more consistent than it is for the linguists. In fact it is not limited to the relation among the elements of language (among phonemes, between *signifiant* and *signifié*, among words on the syntagmatic axis and paradigmatic axis), but extends beyond this to concern the dialogic consistency of discourse.

In Bakhtin's writings, linguistic value coincides with dialogic value and, therefore, it can be measured in terms of the word's capacity for dialogicality: not of the formal, surface order, as in the case of an exchange of rejoinders between two speakers in a dialogue, but *substantial* dialogicality, which may even be traced in the voice of a single speaker, in a single utterance.

Through such concepts Bakhtin overcame the conventional limits of linguistics in the direction of what he chose to call "metalinguistics". What he proposes then is not a quantitative extension of the boundaries of linguistics but a qualitative change, a shift in values: the value of sign *identity* is replaced by the value of sign *otherness*. Such a shift in focus means to search for linguistic value in dialogic relations internal to discourse, in dialogic relations that connect different texts, historical languages, discourse genres, etc. Pushed to high degrees of dialogism, extralocality and displacement as regulated by otherness, linguistic value understood as dialogic value becomes aesthetic value.

According to this approach, the relation between aesthetic value and cognitive value is important as well. It too may be reconducted to the scale of different degrees in dialogism, ranging from a maximum degree in dialogism to a maximum degree in monologism. However, in spite of its potential for innovation and revolution, cognitive discourse cannot reach the high levels of dialogic openness and otherness that instead can be traced in artistic discourse: this is because it is grounded in the category of self, it identifies with the subject of discourse, and is oriented in accordance with a given thesis, a unitary project, a conclusion.

All the same cognitive processes also call for the category of otherness, as Bakhtin underlined in various phases of his research. In *Rabelais and His World*, for example, he shows the importance, for the rise of modern scientific knowledge during the Renaissance, of the fact that official culture opens up to non official culture, to popular, carnivalized culture, and to the grotesque body. This point of view is also developed by Bakhtin in his later writings, especially "From Notes Made in 1970-71". And from this point of view, artistic experimentation pushes beyond the scientific, enabling one to understand aspects of humanity (as says Bakhtin in relation to Dostoevsky's "polyphonic novel"), of experience with the other and with nature that are altogether inaccessible in a monological perspective.

The problem of value is a constant concern throughout Bakhtin's research from his early writings of the 1920s to his later writings of the 1970s. Furthermore, given the interdisciplinary perspective of his work with its special focus on the *sense of value for the human person*, Bakhtin's interest in the question of value is not limited to the specific field of a given human science (for example, linguistics, theory of art and literature). By contrast to linguistics of Saussurean derivation, Russian formalism and Lotman's cultural semiotics, for Bakhtin the question of value could not be explained in terms of relations with a closed system, whether a linguistic code, *langue*, so-called "poetic language", or an overall cultural system. All the same, however, for Bakhtin too the problem of specificity and value in verbal signs, literature and cultural texts was fundamental. Bakhtin's perspective is radically dialogic: interlingualism, intertextuality, and interculturalism are important implications of his dialogic principle. Consequently, rather than limit his research on values to the boundaries of a single human science, he searched for the unitary sense for the human person subtending the division itself of the sciences.

All this has consequences on the method used by Bakhtin throughout the whole course of his research: it consists in relating fields and objects of study, that would seem to be distant from each other, through a process of shifting and opening, rather than of englobement and closure. This method is dialectic in a strong sense insofar as it recovers the connection with dialogism, which is fundamental in obtaining dialectics; this is the dialogic-dialectic method, or "detotalizing method".

Bakhtin placed the prefix "meta" in front of the word "linguistics" (in *Problems of Dostoevsky's Poetics*) to describe his particular approach to verbal language; in fact this prefix may be appropriately extended to all fields involved in his research, which he considered as properly philosophical insofar as it is critical research focusing on conditions of possibility. As regards the problematic of values and of the signs through which they are necessarily expressed (which leads to Bakhtin's interest in the general science of signs or semiotics), the metalinguistic approach means to develop a theoretical perspective as well as a guide to practice which rather than absolutize and reify signs and values, inquires into the dialectic-dialogic processes of their production and circulation.

If by "philosophy of language" we intend (when a question of verbal language) a study that turns its attention to the inherently philosophical dimension of language and, therefore, to the philosophical founding of language, and not the reduction of philosophical problems to problems of (verbal) language, the work of Bakhtin and his Circle is a fundamental point of reference. Bakhtin trascended the limits of traditional approaches to the study of language, which were centred on the centripetal forces operating in the verbal and nonverbal sign network and made to converge in monological, fixed units. On the contrary, he oriented philosophy of language according to the live values of otherness, dialogicality and extralocality which figure as the end and founding principles both of signfying processes and of the sciences that study them. Consequently, contrary to currents that reduce philosophy of language to problems of language and separate them from the live context of social communication understood in terms of understanding (which is always to a certain extent "dialogic comprehension", and answerability to the other), Bakhtin conceived philosophy of language as theory of knowledge, praxis and ideology developed in the light of a theory of language at once critical and dialogic.

As we have seen, a fundamental characteristic of Bakhtin's linguistic theory is its interdisciplinary perspective. Bakhtin considered language in relation to the languages of the other human sciences (in turn made of dialogic relations) including anthropology, psychology, psychoanalysis, theory of ideology, the study of popular traditions and of different socio-cultural systems and practices, linguistics and theory of literature, all of which converge in the dialogic and critical orientation of his theory of language. However, Bakhtin drew on literature in particular for his understanding of language on the basis of his convinction that literary language is the place which most exalts and manifests the live characteristics of communication, the "word's" plurivocality, its "dialogized plurilingualism", structural not only to the relation between different discourses but also to the discourse of a single voice.

Bakhtinian theory of literary language is constructed through dialogic confrontation with the variegated horizon of different languages. Consequently, the practices, theories, values and orientations of other sciences connected to language because they deal with language or simply because language is the material they are made of, all enter Bakhtinian theory of literature. All these experiences are made to converge in the live material of literary language and in the centrifugal and contradictory forces operative in it, as the place where the sign manifests its expressive potential to a maximum degree of dialogic answerability. For Bakhtin literary language becomes the model, material and instrument for a critique of those approaches to language theory that do not keep account of language from the point of view of its dialogic, polyphonic and plurivocal constitution.

As we have mentioned, Bakhtin preferred the term "meta-linguistics" to "linguistics" to describe the orientation of his research on language, but we could also add "philosophy of language", to recall the title of the 1929 volume, *Mrxism and the Philosophy of Language,* signed by Voloshinov. Bakhtin's research centres particularly on the problem of the specificity of the literary word, which he dealt with on the basis of his reflections on language and word, conducted along the borders of diverse disciplines, along their junctures and points of intersection where both verbal and nonverbal signs come into play. His basic unit of analysis is the utterance as obtained in the internal and external dialogic relations forming speech acts, texts, discourse genres. Thus understood the problem of understanding the utterance exceeds the limits of linguistics:

> The problem of understanding the utterance. In order to understand, it is first of all necessary to establish the principal and clear-cut boundaries of the utterance. The alternation of speech subjects. The ability to determine the response. The essential responsiveness of any understanding ("*Kannitverstan*") (Bakhtin 1959-61, Eng. trans.: 112).

Contrary to those linguistic analyses which search for meaning in unitary, well-defined entities, forgetting the live nature of the processes of signification and communication, Bakhtin defines the "boundaries" of the utterance in terms of the relation among subjects, with reference to the response elicited by the utterance and to the responsive nature of understanding: in other words, the "boundaries" of the utterance coincide with the dialogic interrelationship with the utterance, the text. Therefore, the utterance is an open, dialogic, intertextual unit whose signifying value is determined in its contact with the other. Bakhtin gave first importance to the dynamical and creative forces of real linguistic life, and this led him to conduct his linguistic analysis of the utterance in the broad context of its relations with the other human sciences. The boundaries of the utterance understood as a dialogic unit are open and in continual construction in the relation with the outside, the other, with respect to which the utterance finds its sense. Given his special interest for the verbal text considered in relation to nonverbal texts (cf. Bakhtin 1965), Bakhtin himself, as mentioned, qualified his research as "philosophical",

> mainly because of what it is not: it is not a linguistic, philological, literary, or any other special kind of analysis (study). The advantages are these: our study will move in the liminal spheres, that is, on the borders of all the aforementioned disciplines; at their junctures and points of intersection (Bakhtin 1959-61, Eng. trans. : 103).

However, Bakhtin's considerations in this direction can in fact be traced back to earlier writings with respect to his 1959-61 paper. He had already formulated his critique of "abstract objectivism" characteristic of certain approaches in philosophy of language, and of "individualistic subjectivism" in general linguistics, in his books with Voloshinov of 1927 and 1929. Such critique is the starting point and premise which sets the orientation for all Bakhtin's research on the word and the sign in general. But let us consider the following passage from *Problems of Dostoevsky's Poetics* (the first edition was published in 1929) as a possible example among the many clearly illustrating Bakhtin's "metalinguistic", or if we prefer, "metasemiotical" approach:

> [...] linguistics studies "language" itself and the logic specific to it in its capacity as a *common ground*, as that which *makes possible* dialogic interaction; consequently, linguistics distances itself from the actual dialogic relationships themselves. These relationships lie in the realm of discourse, for discourse is by its very nature dialogic; they must therefore be studied by metalinguistics, which exceeds the limits of linguistics and has its own independent subject matter and tasks.
>
> Dialogic relationships are reducible neither to logical relationships nor to relationships oriented semantically toward their referential object, *relationships in and of themselves* devoid of any dialogic element. They must clothe themselves in discourse, become utteraces, become the positions of various subjects expressed in discourse, in order that dialogic relationships might arise among them (Bakhtin 1963, Eng. trans.: 183).

In order to undersand Bakhtin's approach to studies on verbal language we must remember his insistance on the inexorable connection between literary language and life, which is direct and dialectic. Literary language is grounded in the heterogeneous material of life establishing relations between alterities, between the *other* of literature, or art in general, and the *other* of life which literature renders by taking its distances from it according to the principle of extralocality. Bakhtin theorizes dialogic understanding among alterities which encounter each other in the dialectic unity of responsibility/answerability understood in terms of listening to the other, of responsivity to the other. Art and life do not identify with each other: the irreducible otherness of life, its polyphony, resounds in the language of art, and life is the material of art in which life itself is enhanced and in turn nurtures. As says Bakhtin in "Art and Answerability":

> But what guarantees the inner connection of the constituent elements of a person? Only the unity of answerability. I have to answer with my own life for what I have experienced and understood in art, so that everything I have experienced and understood would not remain ineffectual in my life. [...]. The poet must remember that it is his poetry which bears the guilt for the vulgar prose of life, whereas the man of everyday life ought to know that the fruitlessness of art is due to his willingness to be unexact-

ing and to the unseriousness of the concerns in his life (Bakhtin 1919, Eng. trans.: 1-2).

For a new approach to philosophy of language which keeps account of Bakhtin's theory of literature, the relation evidenced between art and life (which must never be forgotten in philosophy) is fundamental. Bakhtin shows how Dostoevsky's artistic world revolves around dialogue considered as an end and not as a means, and, in accordance with Dostoevsky, he even goes as far as identifying in dialogue the material itself of human becoming:

> Dialogue here is not the threshold to action, it is the action itself. It is not a means for revealing, for bringing to the surface the already ready-made character of a person; no, in dialogue a person not only shows himself outwardly, but he becomes for the first time that which he is — and, we repeat, not only for others but for himself as well. To be means to communicate dialogically (Bakhtin 1963, Eng. trans.: 252).

Language, the subject, consciousness, values, orientations, ideologies are all dialogic and social constructs built on the borders and junctures uniting internal and external alterities:

> I am conscious of myself and become myself only while revealing myself for another, through another, and with the help of another [...]. And everything internal gravitates not toward itself but is turned to the outside and dialogized, every internal experience ends up on the boundary, encounters another, and in this tension-filled encounter lies its entire essence [...]. The very being of man (both external and internal) is the *deepest communion. To be* means *to communicate* (Bakhtin 1961, Eng. trans.: 287).

To practice philosophy of language in a Bakhtinian perspective implies grasping the philosophical instance of language through the experience of literature which, in turn, presupposes this instance. The philosophical dimension of language, but we might add "ethical" dimension insofar as it is determined by the value of otherness and extralocality, is the immanent disposition of language itself to transcend its own limits (as well as the limits of life as expressed and produced in it), according to the logic of dialogized and plurilinguistic otherness (being the condition for signifying and communication processes), and not of identity and equal exchange. In the Bakhtinian perspective, the theory of literary language and the philosophical theory of language encounter each other: both open to the ethical dimension, that is, the plurivocal and dialogic otherness characterizing the universes of human discourse. Differently to the specialized language of the sciences, on one hand, and with reference to literary language, on the other, especially Dostoevsky's polyphonic novel, it becomes clear that the specificity of philosophical language lies in its plurilingualism, pluristylism and pluridiscursivity.

Philosophy of language must not ignore the correlation between philosophy and literature if, as anticipated at the beginning of this paper, "rather than reduce philosophical problems to problems of language, it is to focus on the philosophical grounding of language, beginning from the problem of the language of philosophy" (Ponzio 1994: 193). To place philosophy alongside literature, especially the novelistic genre in its polyphonic variant, as does Bakhtin, may seem arbitrary. Indeed, this procedure involves relating two things that are different: on one side, a dimension, an attitude, an orientation, which as such cuts across all discourses, at least potentially, beyond the limits of genre, flowing into the novel as well; on the other, a specific discourse genre. However, this discrepancy is easily overcome if we take our distances from a hypostatizing vision of literary genres, and consider the genre as an "interpretative model of reality" (Bakhtin 1938; see also Bakhtin-Voloshinov 1929, Part Three, Chapters 2 + 3; Medvedev 1928, Eng. trans.: 130-131), as a "modelling procedure" or "specific signifying procedure" (cf. Ponzio 1994: 58-66).

Of literary genres, the novel reaches the highest degrees of pluridiscursivity and plurivocality in language; at a metalinguistic level it is the genre that best renders such orientations. As demonstrated by Bakhtin (cf. 1934-35), the sciences of language —including philosophy of language, linguistics, stylistics and philology— do not dispose of equally adequate instruments for an understanding of such orientations. They refer to the logic of identity, to the centripetal forces operating in the system of language, to monologism, to the processes of identification which are made to prevail over the processes of dialogic and responsive understanding, to the historical processes of linguistico-ideological unification and centralization, all of which reduce the complex life of language to polarization between the unitary system of language, on one hand, and individual use of this system, on the other.

Bakhtin, together with other scholars of language, of signifying and communication processes in general, such as Edmund Husserl, Charles S. Peirce, Ferruccio Rossi-Landi, Roland Barthes, Maurice Blanchot, Emmanuel Lévinas are the main interlocutors in a dialogue proposed by Augusto Ponzio in his book, *Fondamenti di filosofia del linguaggio*, 1994, as part of his project for the development of a new approach to philosophy of language. (It is no incident that this book is preceded by a series of monographs by Ponzio on Rossi-Landi, Lévinas and Bakhtin; for a more detailed description, see Petrilli 1996a: 229-242). Similarly to Bakhtin as regards the word in the novel, Ponzio identifies dialogicality as a special characteristic of the language of philosophy. And, indeed, the juncture between the word in the novel and the philosophical word is traceable on a genetic level. Bakhtin shows how the "polyphonic novel" genre originates from "Socratic dialogue". The latter, in turn, is grounded in the carnivalesque orientation of popular culture which contrasts the joyous relativity of a topsy turvy world with the monologism, univocality and dogmatism of hegemonic culture (cf. Bakhtin 1963, Eng. trans.: 106-114). *Fondamenti* is a contribution to Bakhtin's project for the development of philosophy of language based on the ethics of otherness and dialogism:

> Thanks to its vocation for dialogized pluridiscursivity, philosophy cannot ignore those places of language where the dialogic life of the word is developed, where outside the philosophical sphere too, the word is experimented through provocation by another word, where speech resounds as pluristylistic, pluridiscursive and plurivocal. Among the places of dialogization special mention must be made of the parodic and "carnivalized" genres of the oral and written traditions, of all forms of literary writing where indirect speech and extralocality render the word self-critical, self-derisive, capable of not taking itself seriously, a word that is internally dialogic [...] (Ponzio 1994: 195).

Philosophical reflection on verbal and nonverbal language favours development of a detotalizing approach to the various fields of knowledge, praxis and human values considered in terms of sign material. No claim is made to totalization or semiotico-philosophical imperialism. The "detotalizing" method of inquiry evidences the ethical dimension of language and communication in addition to the aesthetic dimension, thanks above all to results obtained through experimentation of the word's dialogic potential in the laboratory of literary writing.

References

Bakhtin, Mikhail M.

1919 "Art and Answerability (1919)", in Bakhtin 1979, Eng. trans. 1990, pp. 1-3.

1920-23 "Author and Hero in Aesthetic Activity", in Bakhtin 1979, Eng. trans. 1990, pp. 4-256.

1934-35 "Discourse in the Novel", in Bakhtin 1975, Eng. trans. 1981, pp. 259-422.

1938 "Epic and the Novel", in Bakhtin 1975, Eng. trans. 1981, pp. 3-40.

1959-61 "The Problem of the Text in Linguistics, Philology, and the Human Sciences: An Experiment in Philosophical Analysis", in Bakhtin 1975, Eng. trans. 1986, pp. 103-131.

1961"Toward a Reworking of the Dostoevsky Book", in Bakhtin 1979, Eng. trans. in Bakhtin, *Problems of Dostoevsky's Poetics (1929),* Eng. trans. and ed. by C. Emerson, University of Minnesota Press, Minneapolis, Minn., 1984, pp. 283-302.

1963 *Problems of Dostoevsky's Poetics (1929),* Eng. trans. and ed. by C. Emerson, University of Minnesota Press, Minneapolis, Minn., 1984.

1965 *Rabelais and His World,* Eng. trans. H. Iswolsky, Indiana University Press, Bloomington, Indiana, 1984.

1970-71 "From Notes Made in 1970-71", in Bakhtin 1979, Eng. trans. 1986, pp. 132-158.

1974 "Toward a Methodology for the Human Sciences", in Bakhtin 1979, Eng. trans. 1986, pp. 159-172.

1975 *Voprosy literatury i estetiki,* Chudozestvennaja literatura, Moscow.

1979 *Estetika slovesnogo tvorčestva,* Iskusstvo, Moscow.

1981 *The Dialogic Imagination by M.M. Bakhtin,* ed. by M. Holquist, trans. by C. Emerson and M. Holquist, University of Texas Press, Austin, 1981.

1986 *Speech Genres & Other Late Essays,* trans. by V. McGee, ed. by C. Emerson and M. Holquist, University of Texas Press, Austin.

1990 *Art and Answerability. Early Philosophical Essays by M.M. Bakhtin,* ed. by M. Holquist and V. Liapunov, trans. and notes by V. Liapunov, suppl. trans. by K. Brostrom, University of Texas Press, Austin, 1990.

1993 *Toward a Philosophy of the Act,* trans. and notes by V. Liapunov, ed. by M. Holquist & V. Liapunov, University of Texas Press, Austin; It. trans. in Bakhtin 1995, pp. 43-100.

1995 (in collab. with Kangev, Medvedev, Voloshinov) *Bachtin e le sue maschere. Il percorso bachtiniano fino ai Problemi dell'opera di Dostoevskij (1919-1929),* ed. by A. Ponzio, P. Jachia, M. De Michiel, Dedalo, Bari.

1997 *Hacia una filosofía del acto ético. De los borradores y otros escritos,* Comentarios de Iris M. Zavala y Augusto Ponzio, trad. del ruso de T. Bubnova, Anthropos, Barcelona; Editorial de la Universidad de Puerto Rico, San Juan.

1998 *Per una filosofia dell'azione responsabile,* con due saggi di Augusto Ponzio e Iris M. Zavala, trans. from 2nd Russian ed. by M. De Michiel, Piero Manni, Lecce.

Bakhtin, Mikhail M.; Medvedev, Pavel N.

1928 *The Formal Method in Literary Scholarship: A Critical Introduction to Sociological Poetics,* Eng. trans. by A.J. Wehrle, The Johns Hopkins University Press, Baltimore, Md., 1978.

Bakhtin, Mikhail M.; Voloshinov, Valentin N.

1926 "Discourse in Life and Discourse in Poetry: Questions of Sociological Poetics", Eng. trans. by J. Richmond, in *Bakhtin School Papers*, ed. by A. Shukman, RPT, Publications Somerton, Oxford and Dept. of Lit., Univ. of Essex, Colchester, 1988, pp. 5-30.

1927 *Freudianism: A Critical Sketch*, trans. by I.R. Titunik, ed. by I.R.Titunik with N.H.Bruss, Indiana University Press, Indianapolis, Indiana, 1987.

1929 *Marxism and the Philosophy of Language*, Eng. trans. by L. Matejka and I.R. Titunik, Harvard University Press, Cambridge (Mass.), 1976; It. trans. from the English, *Marxismo e filosofia del linguaggio*, Dedalo, Bari, 1976; but see also Bakhtin-Voloshinov 1999.

1999 *Marxismo e filosofia del linguaggio*, ed. & pres. by A. Ponzio, trans. from Russian and intro. by M. De Michiel, Piero Manni, Lecce.

Petrilli, Susan

1990a "Dialogue and Chronotopic Otherness: Bakhtin and Welby", *Discours social/Social Discourse*, 3, (1/2), pp. 339-350.

1990b "The Problem of Signifying in Welby, Peirce, Vailati, Bakhtin", in A. Ponzio 1990a, pp. 313-363.

1990c "On the Materiality of Signs", in A. Ponzio 1990a, pp.365-392.

1992a "The Detotalizing Method, Human Sciences and the Dialogic of Values", *Social Semiotics*, 2/2, pp. 98-113.

1992b "Translation, semiotics and ideology", *TTR. Etudes sur le texte et ses transformations*, V, 1, pp. 223-264.

1993a "Signs and Values: for a Critique of Cognitive Semiotics", *Journal of Pragmatics*, 20, pp. 239-251.

1993b "Dialogism and Interpretation in the Study of Signs", *Semiotica*, 97-1/2, pp. 103-118.

1993c see Ponzio 1993a.

1995 *Materia segnica e interpretazione*, Milella, Lecce.

1996a *Che cosa significa significare?* Edizioni dal Sud, Bari.

1996b "Bakhtin Read in Italy (1980-1994)", *Le Bulletin Bachtin / The Bakhtin Newsletter* 5, pp. 55-66.

1996c "Bachtin in Italia negli ultimi quindici anni (1985-1995)", *L'immagine riflessa* V, pp. 47-71.

1997 "Bachtin in Italia negli ultimi quindici anni (1985-1995)", in A. Ponzio 1997a, pp. 311-340; updated version of Petrilli 1996c.

1998a *Teoria dei segni e del linguaggio*, Graphis, Bari.

1998b *Su Victoria Welby. Significs e filosofia del linguaggio*, Edizioni Scientifiche Italiane, Naples.

1999 see Ponzio 1999a.

Ponzio, Augusto

1980 *Michail Bachtin. Alle origini della semiotica sovietica*, Dedalo, Bari.

1985 (in collab. with M.A. Bonfantini & G. Mininni), *Per parlare dei segni/ Talking About Signs*, Eng. trans. by S. Petrilli, Adriatica, Bari.

1988 *Ferruccio Rossi-Landi e la filosofia del linguaggio*, Adriatica, Bari.

1989 *Soggetto e alterità. Da Lévinas a Lévinas*, con un'intervista a Lévinas, Adriatica, Bari, 1st ed. 1983.

1990a *Man as a Sign. Essays on the Philosophy of Language*, ed. and trans. by S. Petrilli, Mouton De Gruyter, Berlin.

1990b "Bakhtinian Alterity and the Search for Identity in Europe Today", *Discours social/Social Discourse*, 3, (1/2), pp. 217-228.

1992 *Tra semiotica e letteratura. Introduzione a Michail Bachtin*, Bompiani, Milan.

1993a (in collab. with O. Calabrese and S. Petrilli), *La ricerca semiotica*, Esculapio, Bologna.

1993b *Signs, Dialogue and Ideology*, Eng. trans. by S. Petrilli, John Benjamins, Amsterdam.

1994 (in collab. with P. Calefato & S. Petrilli), *Fondamenti di filosofia del linguaggio*, Laterza, Bari, new ed. 1999.

1995 *Segni per parlare di segni/Signs to Talk About Signs*, Eng. trans. by S. Petrilli, Adriatica, Bari.

1996 *Sujet et altérité. Sur Emmanuel Lévinas*, suivi de Deux dialogues avec Emmanuel Lévinas, L'Harmattan, Paris.

1997a *La rivoluzione bachtiniana. Il pensiero di Bachtin e l'ideologia contemporanea*, Levante Editore, Bari; Spanish edition, *La revolución Bajtiniana. El pensamiento de Bajtín y la ideología contemporánea*, trans. by M. Arriaga, Frónesis Cátedra, Univesitat de València, Madrid, 1998.

1997b "Para una filosofia de la acción", in M. M. Bakhtin 1997, pp. 225-246.

1999 *La comunicazione*, Graphis, Bari.

Ponzio, Augusto; Petrilli, Susan

1998 *Signs of Research on Signs*, *Semiotische Berichte* Jg. 22, 3, 4.

1999 *Fuori campo. I segni del corpo tra rappresentazione ed eccedenza*, Mimesis, Milan.

2000 *Il sentire della comunicazione globale*, Meltemi, Rome.

Saussure, Ferdinand de

1916 *Cours de linguistique générale*, ed. by Ch. Bally and A. Séchehaye, Payot, Paris, 1964; critical ed. by R. Engler, Wiesbaden, Otto Harrassowitz, 4 voll., 1968-1974.

Vygotsky, Lev S.
1925 "Soznanie kak problema psichologii povedenija", in K.N. Kornilov (ed.), *Psichologija i marksizm*, Moscow/Leningrad, 1925.